# THE PHILOSOPHER SAVANT

## RUSTIN LARSON

GLASS LYRE PRESS

Copyright © 2015 Rustin Larson
Paperback ISBN: 978-1-941783-12-2

All rights reserved: except for the purpose of quoting brief passages for review, no part of this book may be reproduced or transmitted in any form or by any means, electronic or mechanical, including photocopying, recording, or by any information storage and retrieval system, without permission in writing from the publisher.

Cover art: "Inner Landscape #3" by Caroline Larson
Design & layout: Steven Asmussen
Copyediting: Linda E. Kim
Author Photo: G. Watt

Glass Lyre Press, LLC
P.O. Box 2693
Glenview, IL 60026

www.GlassLyrePress.com

# Contents

| | |
|---|---|
| ...Stays Home from Church | 9 |
| ...Remembers a Reunion, 1956 | 10 |
| ...Visualizes a Past Incarnation and Death as a Pioneer Woman | 11 |
| ...Contemplates the Old Man Crying | 12 |
| ...Contemplates the Funny Papers | 13 |
| ...Contemplates Peanut Butter | 14 |
| ...Contemplates Bones | 15 |
| ...Takes a Walk | 16 |
| ...Asks "Should We Have Gone Back?" | 17 |
| ...Contemplates a Monument | 18 |
| ...Contemplates the Federal City | 19 |
| ...Contemplates Notes | 20 |
| ...Contemplates the Only Highway We Can Think of | 21 |
| ...Contemplates the Dangerous Sun | 22 |
| ...Contemplates the Ox-Bow Lake | 23 |
| ...Writes a Letter to Kindness | 24 |
| ...Knew for Certain You Were Never Coming Back | 25 |
| ...Dresses His Dad for His Funeral | 26 |
| ...Contemplates Oblivion | 27 |
| ..Contemplates His Imagined Abandonment as a Child | 28 |
| ...Visualizes a Mechanical Angel | 29 |
| ...Dreams of War | 30 |
| ...Contemplates a Summer Evening | 31 |
| ...Again Dreams of War | 32 |
| ...Reconsiders the Presidency of Richard Milhous Nixon | 33 |
| ...Smiles at the Ghost of John Keats | 34 |
| ...Thinks of Ophelia | 35 |
| ...Contemplates Curtains | 36 |

| | |
|---|---|
| ...Contemplates an Exposed Fossil Bed Near Iowa City | 37 |
| ...Dreams of the Flood | 38 |
| ...Remembers the August Garage | 39 |
| ...Sees the Sparrow Dancing | 40 |
| ...Goes East Down Burlington | 41 |
| ...Considers the Wax Inside the Orchid | 42 |
| ...Empathizes with How the Woman in the White Peugeot Returns | 43 |
| ...Recalls the Marching Band | 44 |
| ...Empathizes with How the Woman in the White Peugeot Drives Without Shadows | 45 |
| ...Empathizes with How the Woman of the White Peugeot Practices | 46 |
| ...Empathizes with the Solitary Child | 47 |
| ...Acknowledges Winter Again | 48 |
| ...Dreamed He Had Died | 49 |
| ...Watches a Space Drama | 50 |
| ...Wakes Up as Usual | 51 |
| ...Hears a Spring Song | 52 |
| ...Hears Piano Music Climbing, 9:41 PM | 53 |
| Acknowledgments | 57 |
| About the Author | 59 |

*To the fathers. You tried, you poor blokes.*

# The Philosopher Savant Stays Home from Church

Sitting quietly with philodendrons,
Filling out the forms
The ticking clock slides
Over the table.
Taking a sip of cold tea,
Burning down the house,
And taking a walk in the snow
While everyone else prays.
Buying chocolate at a gas station,
Hitchhiking to the middle
Of the hills
Where few people live,
Kicking the carcass
Of a deer on the gravel shoulder,
A flashing in my eyes,
I arrive at a mansion
Surrounded by fallen branches
And ice.
Inside are chairs
That resemble lions
Or laws
Or the boredom of kings.
A piano,
With its keys locked under its cover,
Is some giant creature
At the bottom of the sea,
Waiting.

## The Philosopher Savant Remembers a Reunion, 1956

The two-toned Buick parked in the sycamore shade,
The drive made of powdery dust, the weeds feathery
Beneath your feet; let the trees sigh where they are,
And the shadows mark the beginning of our lives.
Let the grown-ups smoke their disappointments
To the filters and throw them glowing
Into the grasses; let the godmother speak nothing
But French; let the uncles gorge themselves
On cold cuts and beer snapped open by the angry beak
Of the what'sittooya bird. There are no other farms
Like this one. The country rushes out to devour
Every faint whisper.

# The Philosopher Savant
## Visualizes a Past Incarnation and Death as a Pioneer Woman

Then night came and I thought of flowers,
And back again, and closed in memory,
Their blue petals inward and drunk; I'd lie
And think and see fire-stormed earth,
A bright field of humming flies. The birth
Of flowers in their doorstep shade. "What's left?"
They ask, open slowly, bereft.
I always thought flowers were women,
A dress tapering into the new sun. These hands
Pick the fire flowers, darkness in part,
Sun in the other. Close the cabinet,
Cover my earth. Shovel on the rich heart,
Crown star, traveler's joy, blazing vetch.

# The Philosopher Savant Contemplates the Old Man Crying

The locomotives are steam; bells are clanking;
A great swarm of people rises from the clouds,
Floats down the platform, floats right through me,
Seeing nothing. At the newsstand, I see the ghost
Of my father. "Why are you crying?" I ask.

The translucent old man and his wolf watch
The moon rise above the blue-green ocean.
Precisely eight lavender clouds fly low over
The waves. "How many fish do you suppose
Are in the ocean?" The old man asks his wolf.

My father would read the funny papers to me on Sunday.
He wore a T-shirt and smelled like pancakes. I would ask him
What Rex Morgan MD was all about. And he would say,
"Ah, nothing. Crazy stuff."

# The Philosopher Savant Contemplates the Funny Papers

It occurred to me that I am not my father. I read the funny papers
This morning. It was nothing. Crazy stuff. Some of the comics
Had been there fifty years or more. The children were not older.
Some were still in pajamas and had heads like peaches.

A flock of geraniums lies outside the apple tree. The sundial catches
The sun's rays. Shadow tells the time. The geraniums cluster
Like churchgoers. The apples were poor and rotted this year.
I've come 100 miles. The tree offers glints of white. Its branches

Are hypnotism. I scared my mother by crawling into
A waste basket and playing dead. She blew
Into my nostrils to wake me up. The walls laughed yellow.
It was this day. It was fifty years ago.

# The Philosopher Savant Contemplates Peanut Butter

My brother climbed the elm tree with a peanut butter sandwich
And a saw. I called him peanut butter boy. He cried.
The limb came down with a crash. My mother accused him. I turned
Into a branch. Two branches. The branches became Icarus wings.
I jumped from the sun and fell to our patio. Our Boston Terrier
Licked the salt from my face. Reading Proust I understand how
One small space can be rotated and reinvented through walks,
Slow rides in carriages. Look at the church spires.
Strange voice. Feeling ill in the morning, I sit and wait.

# The Philosopher Savant Contemplates Bones

They had moved here so the father could take a job
As a math teacher. They had three boys. One day,
Digging, in the exuberance of play,

One of the boys unearthed the bones of a dog.
They had forgotten where they had buried their pet.
The boys gathered around the bones and wept.

We buried my dad in a pretty cheap casket.
It was a decision made between my brothers and me.
Would a prettier coffin have eased anyone's conscience?

A color guard from the navy came.
I saluted and felt pretty damned silly. It was 2001,
In November, so 9-11 was still crisp
In the memory. A color guard from the navy came:
My father's bones closed in a wooden ship.

# The Philosopher Savant Takes a Walk

On my way to the post office this morning, I was feeling
Pretty balanced, pretty good. I looked at the movie posters;
I passed the tattoo-and-piercing establishment. Some
Restaurant was frying up a batch of onions.
I got over that and kept walking. I retrieved my mail.
If I can be someone's entertainment by being myself,
I have no regrets. I believed in my footsteps. I crossed
To walk through the gazebo. There were a few marigolds.
The sun was tilted and coolly golden. A crippled woman
Watched me from her car. It was a Tuesday; I remember that much.

## The Philosopher Savant Asks "Should We Have Gone Back?"

Should we have gone back to the poisons flowering in the hedges?
Should we have grounded in an embankment and listened to the cardinals
of our accident embroider the gangrened earth, our tooth
scattered engagement, of our sexless death? Should we have gone
back? She stood there waving from the kitchen screen, our lullaby in faded

Gingham, eyes like cherries the robins had pecked. Oh, what did she see
about our skeletons she couldn't tell earlier, seanced around her table
with stupefying tumblers of Southern Comfort and gelatin eyes of ice.
Should we have gone back to the birds burning the world? To the birds
burning the world with their advice.

# The Philosopher Savant Contemplates a Monument

Someone threw a brick into the middle
Of my yard—someone, self-
Monumentizing, chose a lump
Of red, man-made stone to be
Remembered by, though no personal
Name or date is attached—but
The mere presence of the thing
In my clump of clover says, "Listen,
Whoever I was, I was here, and
Your yard I chose as the memorial
To everything I hold and held dear."
The man-made stone stays there.
Not even half a brick, so portable, so
Easy to throw, it has no better place to go.

# The Philosopher Savant Contemplates the Federal City

*Because I had a passion* pours a glass of orange juice, sits
with a stack of smudged newspapers. *Because
I'm afraid of ridicule* is here with me in the shadows of my ink. *If I only
had loved a square of me* is still riding
the bus to high school, hands quivering, knowing
the day of death has come for the sparrows.
*Can I have a dollar* is at a different subway station in time. She is young
and I have doubts she will live beyond seven-
teen, begging for pocket change on 11th
in Washington. I turn to her, ghost that she is, daughter I never had.
*Thistle in abandoned lots, medicine of a change that didn't happen,*
nothing I could have done short tossing my soul
into a plate of kerosene, chased by the tracer of a cigarette,
would have been adequate. Invisible crowds
rushing to Federal City, I too was young, please remember, 23, holding
a fresh leather briefcase the lies of time
wash over eternally; I left you, not even a wish to light your way out.

# The Philosopher Savant Contemplates Notes

Arteries of a strange heart. Blue sky. Bare
black branches. There is an apartment I
don't live in. They condemned the building;
no one is supposed to live there now. Once,
in my bedroom, I sat with my copy
of Hart Crane, trying to get the size
of the poem. Sometimes I walk there, sneak in,
stand in that empty room. Coat hangers scattered
all over the floor just as I left it.

I dreamt I sat with some guru; he was
explaining to me, calmly, the transition
between incarnations; how past identities
might surface; how to remain unperturbed
and move forward. One of the embellished,
one of the endlessly repeated. I listen
to John Coltrane, a song performed three years
before I was born. 1956.
On a Misty Night. A jungle gym: notes
around an almost familiar melody.
"But then, suddenly," the liner reads, "John
Coltrane was dead." The music is unthinkably real.

## The Philosopher Savant Contemplates the Only Highway we Can Think of

I listen to my daughters sing.
The washing machine chugs
us far onto the sea, the stars
above us, the wind cold yet scented:
the balsam of incalculable shores.
"I have serious homework to do," Sarah
says, warning her sister, "so if you are
to stay in my room you have to be
absolutely quiet." The world outside
obliges. The sea of night full of nothing
but strangeness—the vertigo of the lifting
and smothering of waves—
past the Grand Banks and the lovesick boys
and the earthworms, say the sisters in their
utter silence. The stars like lanterns
of lonely wives; the wind, the robes of ghosts
fluttering from and around us:
so many missions. The sisters' tea
cups tinkle like muffled bells. The life of water
darkens into the only road we see.

# THE PHILOSOPHER SAVANT
# CONTEMPLATES THE DANGEROUS SUN

The tinsel under which I showered this morning
kissed my cold closed eyes and made me shine
sadly. The soap that fragranced my thoughts
and hair rode on my skin
in the car on the street of the miniature city
through which I clattered humbly
to my cross and grave and otherwise euphonic
emblem of a job.
Later, at the Army Post Tap, my friend had a great tribal song
he yelped like a coyote in shadow
purpled into the corners of abandoned
playgrounds, schools, rubble.
The dangerous sun burned itself to sleep.
And that was the only thing that kept me going.
And that is the only thing I love.

# The Philosopher Savant Contemplates the Ox-Bow Lake

Onto the wormy earth, no shoes,
into the bright-beaten patches of mud
and bottle glass, I could dig for treasure:

blind plastic grenadier with his wrinkle
of anguish; blue Indian, his bow
stretched back in vengeance, arrow

poised, a one-way sign down a narrow
road of smartweed to a cul-de-sac of shoes
abandoned with other clothes, the ox-bow

splashing with naked swimmers, orange mud
of clay, undulation, a wrinkle
of sun across the water.

# The Philosopher Savant
# Writes a Letter to Kindness

> *...it is...only kindness that ties your shoes*
> *and sends you out into the day to mail letters and purchase*
> *bread....*
>
> —Naomi Shihab Nye

Before I send my letter to the Great Midwestern Tornado, I tie,
carefully, the laces of my shoes: Silver Spring station, my briefcase
full of mail to strangers who will or will not use these letters to more strangers.

Your words are the purchase-price of another survival—
they are mortal bread I swallow on the streets
of Washington, D.C., communion bread of a whisper.

My shoes do all the thinking on the filthy pavement, on splatters
like letters from a doomed language of concrete.

I send my mail because it is only —what?— that makes sense anymore,
letters I mail directly against "No." I purchase fresh-cut daylilies,
merge the blood of petals and stems with the rain's stuttering flow.

## The Philosopher Savant Knew for Certain You Were Never Coming Back

The water sang. I could hear all the fishes burst
the surface oxygen, see them on the docks, early evening,
mother and father talking softly, sitting in their Adirondacks,
no traces of mourning. 1968. The world was new. A dove
ate an olive branch. My mom sang, half-drunk on the dock at night,
"That Ol' Black Magic," frozen daiquiris until the clouds swam.
The water, its chill, its song of disorganized sensation.
Now, the doves have gone to sleep; the crickets chirp softly
in the gardens of kale, chard and dill; fire arches above.

## The Philosopher Savant Dresses His Dad for His Funeral

Autumn, the news insists, has been gentle.
Driving through the endless
to Des Moines, the radio dial's the only thing
keeping me. At the house, a window
into winter, 9:00 a.m. We think maybe we should
dress you like you are going to a game—black
and gold. We change our minds. I find a dignified
white shirt, a sweater, decent socks, blue slacks,
undies. Nearly forgotten in a pile of your belongings:
a photo, 1959; you look like you are singing,
dressed sloppily in a T-shirt, unshaven. It must
have been Sunday morning, the beginning
of fall, the shadow of wings at the door.

## The Philosopher Savant Contemplates Oblivion

With strangers in the back seat, giddy, a disembodied
drive, Washington, spring 1984—we turned south
onto 16th, ordinary as the budding trees of Rock Creek—
the only radio for that moment, the chatter of whoever we were,
you dressed to the nines, riding shotgun in our tiny
Mitsubishi—southbound, heading into the mouth
of traffic, mass population—the stars unseen in the bright
noon sky, unseen and yet somehow felt, known:
what I thought were memories: bubbles
floating and opalescent: the world: the park's trees,
tennis courts, your lilac garments, rainbow skin,
droplets from the blue, the scented breeze.

## The Philosopher Savant Contemplates His Imagined Abandonment as a Child

Pretend they drove away. They didn't care.
Playthings—bear
in a burning wagon, beads of glass

to crash within a circle
of dust. We haunted
the crooked house in the district

of color, smelled the century's
smoke, decaying beams
of oak. The dust breathed. The dust

settled the land. Firelight
in the eyes of pumpkins. The witch's
broom angled against the hearth.

# The Philosopher Savant Visualizes a Mechanical Angel

The sky burning silver, utterly void
Of birds or flies; a fig tree sawn to ground;
The blue blow-balls nodding in tones sangfroid;
Incendiary chords from her church sounding

The scene, the landscape, garden
Without a history. There is no art,
There is blackness, then star-white words. She wanted
To hate him, but she knew it was not his fault.

The woman knelt close and cradled his head;
She had pulled him from the thing.
He had impacted, swathed through flower beds.
Above: machines. He was a man with wings

Who spiraled down in a helpless fall
And burst to flame against her garden wall.

# The Philosopher Savant Dreams of War

Back toward heaven, stalling, soon the birds
Chased each other overhead, circling, diving,
Silent in storms of white, silver, two birds.
Devoid of hue, the garden flowers swaying,

Last night, I dreamed a silent movie: "Wings."
Like lilac sprigs thrown to a mouth of earth
I cannot say this garden's not a thing,
A column of soldiers mown in death,

The garden death grows, the geography
Of close-cropped red. I hold the back of my head.
Without this art, there is no history;
From body bag a foot swings dead.

I click off the Nightly News.
But behold now the lilac that blooms.

## The Philosopher Savant Contemplates a Summer Evening

Breathing aloud, O death, in pure illumination
As Whitman casting no shadow, the garden
Rippling as if he were endless within
Lit on each color, each flower that's been

Despite this awareness, my focus now
On some destiny marred. But it's curious
The jagged detail of eclipse, shadow
So shifted with its world of breezes

And illumination—each leaf, each flight
Flitting under the shadow of the fig.
I pictured a group of blackbirds, a night
Looking at the garden, a green-blue streak

Of sky. The orange-roofed house, the boil
Of potato soup, taste of olive oil.

## The Philosopher Savant Again Dreams of War

Insurgencies on boundaries of garden
Where chives are sacrificed, daylily, blue
Blow-balls, a war, quietly worked, Eden.
Paint pictures, peaceful, full of flowers, true.

I can't tell if I shall. A red bloom. A bloom.
The important thing to remember is
The subject is rather summery. You
Can see that, expendable into wakefulness.

Into the throat of the wolf fall deeper.
As you draw closer, be repelled, draw
The grotesque imitating some pasture
And think it beautiful. If you saw

The hundreds scythed in fields… and just suppose
Your impression is there and juxtaposed.

## The Philosopher Savant Reconsiders the Presidency of Richard Milhous Nixon

Yellow, orange, green, blue, violet, mere dabs
Of color. Red. So many lives upon
Which the sun would be incessant. Dabs.
Rose sharpened for offensive number one.

Why go into the convolutions of
A single flower completely drawn. Van Gogh
Said, "Oh, I know so very well, my love,
Orchid white, and feminine, and just known."

Richard Nixon considered, and then wrote,
As Christmas bombs fell down upon Hanoi,
"Never are things clearer to me, please note,
Than on my mountain top." An infant boy

Burned. Concussions rang the geography.
No single flower is drawn completely.

## The Philosopher Savant Smiles at the Ghost of John Keats

There is an unplanned clarity in wind
As the first cold begins; hardened leaves fly
And gather our losses in their midst.
They slip through empty branches, lift

An utterance like prayer names whispered
Or wept aloud. They ferry footstep echoes
Till they light and hush beneath the sun, and blow
Again, as rain scatters its violent hue, and lightning

Crackles shadow on the battered hulls.
No more gifted wine there is this season
Than the song these hollow vessels lull.
Keats, seated in his grape-vined patio,

Heard these autumn windship songs.
"Ay, where. And why have I thirsted so long?"

## The Philosopher Savant Thinks of Ophelia

Despite the echoes of my voice, the hemlocks vault
And dust blows upon my face:
Disappointed, lost, full of fault.
The breezes curse the branches black.

The invisible towers; the woodpeckers rattle
And a breath of rain hasn't fallen silver.
O, the bruised white hearts of honeysuckle flowers.
Once, in mayapple mud, orange birds quivered

For clouds overhead that bent
The wet grass cool as Ophelia's hair.
But now, how the raspberry
Stings silent among its leaves and fruit.

Who once found a good deal of comfort here?
We once found a great deal of comfort here.

# The Philosopher Savant Contemplates Curtains

"I hung a curtain in the upstairs window," you say.
The wind puts its lips to the house like Alaska;
the Easter eggs have all been found. I could see them play
Scrabble next door through the window. I love night
walks: the old lady reading in her chair near her fake
aquarium; the old dude sweeping up between tables
at the Asian Deli. The candy jars at the pharmacy. The dark
tables at the bookstore/cafe. A cop slows down to show
he is protecting people like us. I start to walk west
on the heaviest street. The lights rattle
like teleportation units. There is no one diving into dumpsters.
A train starts up with a whoop-whoop
like a navy destroyer. I'm not waiting for anyone's reply--
though tomorrow I know I'll check all the in-boxes,
wonder why you said you'd get back to me
when you only really intended to leave me
hanging forever.

# The Philosopher Savant Contemplates an Exposed Fossil Bed Near Iowa City

Afternoon in the spillway, walking. In an empty
lot nearby, six boys play. Over ocean, upon stone,
feeling the texture of a shell, coral, fish bone,
fin. One boy punts it. For that moment the ball floats
in endless blue. The seas became shallow, dried
layer upon layer, ocean sediment, millions
of years, calcified. I can't believe how light
my father is. 88 pounds. We've seen the imprint of a leaf
in mud, a shoe print, a hand. I slide my hands under
his arms, lift him out. We've seen bones in a forest
slowly covered by leaf rot, and then soil. I lift him
to my chest, guide him awkwardly, the bag
of his catheter hooked in my pocket. I help him
into the wheelchair, pulled into pressure
and heat and compacting stone.

## The Philosopher Savant Dreams of the Flood

The ancestral village, and this time
The river is unlocked in a great flood,
Sinking the roadways and swallowing
The limestone cliffs. My uncle and father
Sit in the stone house on the hilltop, chatting
And drinking brands of beer that have, like them,
Died decades ago. "It's looking
Pretty bad for us," I say, still a mortal
But visiting this living room of the departed.
"In your lifetime, how far did the floods
Go?," I ask. My uncle whistles
Like someone slipping on a banana peel
In an old movie, points to the window
Near the sofa where my dad sips a Dubuque Star,
And says, "Right through there, Bud!"
They both laugh, not going anywhere,
Having achieved a very deep level.

# The Philosopher Savant Remembers the August Garage

Inside it was cool and out of the sun
And we would sit at the workbench
And ponder the wires and sockets
And tubes from a ham radio rebuild
Project abandoned some time back
In 1956 or '57. In his (the invisible father's)
Secret file drawers were magazines
Of nude or partially nude women
Repairing the engines of B-17s,
Old crumbling pages that stank of decades
Of tobacco and shithouses. We concluded
That we would take all this stuff,
The tubes, the wires, the solder, the sockets,
The magazines, and the desiccated pack of Luckies,
And build a robot, someone we could turn to
To explain and interpret the planet
As it screeched out of control on its rusted cogs,
Gears, and axis, someone who would kill
On our command and make us sandwiches,
Someone who would read us stories and patrol
The neighborhood with a never-
sleeping electric blues.

# The Philosopher Savant Sees the Sparrow Dancing

A sparrow dances on the rain-wet boards.
Two citizens from the rain-puddle world
Take shelter under a cherry tree in the mist.
Somehow, I think of the Chinese traveler
In the north, leaving a poem in a bowl
Of snow at the temple. Small puddles
Dance with concentric ringlets. I have
No choice as the rain increases. I too can see
Another world in the puddles, a world
Directly opposite ours with a full sky.
I feel as if the air has separated. Children
Swarm the street there and experience forever.
A sparrow, here, looks down into the puddle
As his opposite peers into our world.

# The Philosopher Savant Goes East Down Burlington

Walking east down Burlington, I notice the cops
Have some kid in the back seat of their cruiser
At the "Jet Stop." All police departments
Hire the same guys: six foot
Two, head shaved, mirrored shades. The back
Door of the cruiser is open: the kid can breathe
At least. Cop Clone #1 blocks the kid's path of escape
While Clone #2 talks to headquarters.
The kid looks terrified, a Mexican youth
With a mustache and a Jesus beard. I can feel
His blood pressure from where I wait.

I see a friend in her car and I wave at her clandestinely
As she pauses at the stop sign. She almost
Collides with another car when she pulls away.

Cops seem to shoot first these days.
Monarch butterflies flirt
In the grasses and trees. That is to say, beneath
Every disaster there is a subtle, but palpable, silence.

# The Philosopher Savant Considers the Wax Inside the Orchid

The afterimage of a cumulus is somewhat red
And fills the sky with a perceived lavender mist.
The football coach, an obese man in a yellow shirt,
Struts to his Silverado, drives away projecting
A shower of gravel.   Players and staff wonder
What kind of bug crawled up his ass. Meanwhile,
It's my birthday and I get lots of weird greetings
And messages. The Czech poet tells me
About "The Wax Inside the Orchid." Meanwhile,
The world is in the mood for football, for a little blood.
This is what I get for being born in the crazy path
Of the year. Winged griffins with the head of Walt
Whitman roam the streets and devour hapless evangelists.
Trees confer like mad scientists
Over the body of a crow. There is no viable means
Of escape; not for us;
We've only been to the moon.  Send an empty
Camera out beyond and you receive
Pictures of orchids, their wax burning and creating
Other shapes, planets and suns.

# The Philosopher Savant Empathizes with How the Woman in the White Peugeot Returns

I step cautiously onto the surface of your planet,
Safe inside my Biological Environment Processing Suit
Or B. E. P. S. or what you may call a female body.
The light of this day could be described as "buttershark."
The cement truck beeps when it goes backwards.
I am sorry, but I am not quite a perfect fit.
I break my string of pearls and drink a pint of coffee.
The girls at the Chit-Chat Club ask me if I have been crying,
If it was because of "him." I wear my cutest dress,
Buy some precious shoes. I look like a bow
And a decoration on a cherry cupcake.
I could just eat me up. I do.

## The Philosopher Savant Recalls the Marching Band

A bearded guy in a confederate grey T-shirt,
And with a gut equal to mine, pushes a huffing
And puffing machine across the practice field,
Painting white stripes, guided by a length
Of string stretched taut against the ground.
I remember practice fields, not as a football player
But as a band member, with a cornet
And a polyester uniform with a ridiculous
Black watch guard's helmet.
I could mention the pack of Kools
I had stuffed in my pocket, the butane lighter.
The stripe guy's machine sounds just like
The African Queen churning up the river
Of grass. A cheerleader languishes
Like Katharine Hepburn on the sidelines.
I forget how we choreographed our moves,
But somehow we spelled 1776 with our bodies
And then marched to form a Liberty Bell.

## The Philosopher Savant Empathizes With How the Woman in the White Peugeot Drives Without Shadows

There is a disparaging label for everything
That breathes. [That is why cemeteries are so
Reassuring and quiet.] Is it possible to write
An account of only the happy, bathed
In golden hour light in October, in an orchard,
In a meadow, in a sloping pasture,
In the musical outlines of grapevines at dawn,
Seen from the window of a train,
West of Bethlehem, still half-dreaming
From having not slept? The money holders
Want us to be very afraid. Still, there she flies.
You won't see her on this train. She is speeding
Parallel in her white bullet, green bottles of wine
In her trunk, in her back seat, racing the shadows.
Poor sister, we can't bring you back.
Your father bought all the shadows.
Now, at 33, when you drive into the rising sun,
Your wines slosh, your silk scarves fly,
You hear the sweet clanking music from Bethlehem.
No, those are not the shadows. We are.

# The Philosopher Savant Empathizes With How the Woman of the White Peugeot Practices

This strange body which lies awake while it sleeps,
Which slouches awake against pillows
While it dreams, this egg in which a never-sleeping eye
Waits, watching. Tell me I can walk out into the clover,
That field where I practice and drive
The small white balls to where they can
Not be found, over and over, set, backswing,
Contact, drive, the flight of the orb
Which sees, which sees, the divine arc
Which encompasses the known world
And its hidden languages, the ripping scarves of script
That flow over the bodies of the slain,
Over Pharaoh's army, the scarves of the witches
And their laughter, and the flight of an owl
From the tomb. At the club house, I drink
The potion, the cocktail like a woman of beauty,
Of wealth, of education. Endless hours,
Tell me I can harvest the essence of clover
As do the bees, with you, my sister, my shadow.

# The Philosopher Savant Empathizes with the Solitary Child

It was a summer like this one, overcast much of the time,
On the average, cool, wet. Even in August
You could feel winter building momentum,
Hear it in the voices of birds, the murmurations of starlings
Swirling the sky with their thought patterns and daydreams.
There I was, a lone dot on the playground
In my hooded sweatshirt like some monk.
If the river of birds was a prayer, it was someone else's
Or no one's. I let go like a sawn branch from an elm tree.
I fell and collected the ground with my body.
I turned and watched the clouds swarm
Like rumpled bolts of grey batting, the foundation
For a tapestry hung in front of the altar of the sun,
A mystery in its very persistence, a note held
In an orchestra of brass and silver baritones,
A spell hovering.

# The Philosopher Savant Acknowledges Winter Again

There is something calming about silhouettes,
Leafless trees against the snow. They
Raise a million arms and say, "I give up."
They wave. The wind, music.

I drove all over the city,
Walked in the park's rose garden in January.
All the roses were caged in leaves and chicken wire
Topped with fez caps of snow.

# The Philosopher Savant Dreamed He Had Died

I was waiting for a crow to come
Fly me to the Spirit World,
But all the crows were busy,
So they sent a blue jay instead.
Blue jay grabbed onto the shoulders
Of my soul and started flying.
Up we went. I looked down,
Saw colors streaming from me
Like a scarf. "Let go!"
Croaked the blue jay. "Can't take
Everything. Too heavy."
Oh, my colorful soul-scarf.
The bird pulled upward. Snap! I let go.
The colors rolled away.
We were free, the stars visible before us.

## The Philosopher Savant Watches a Space Drama

The space robot talks to the wall
And the wall opens upon a cascade
Of steam. In the chamber is the head
Of the robot's brother. This is significant.

A tinsmith makes a woman
Completely out of scraps of metal.

Cattle wander through the scene.
Someone says, "I love you."
Says to the mother, "I have
A sweet tooth for pastry."

A kid runs up and kicks the soccer ball
Into the pool filled with cows' milk.
Ker-splash! A futuristic knife
Slices through a planet made entirely
Of pink salt-water taffy.

There are three jars of blue horseshoe
Crabs' blood in the room where
The second robot is being revived.
The planet makes thunder,
Tornadoes, glass, and monks
Singing and drunk on wine.

# The Philosopher Savant Wakes Up as Usual

I could hear crows
Landing on my window ledge last night.
I flicked my light off and didn't sleep.
But in a while I simply passed out.
"Fantastic!" I said about the color of the sky
In a dream I had. I was sitting propped up by pillows.
In real life, there was a period of light snowfall.
I got up once and looked out the window.
It was 2:22 a. m. The parking lot was empty.
The security light blinked out. Another train
Rumbled through.

## The Philosopher Savant Hears a Spring Song

The walking onions, full of blood,
Are waking up, up and down the street
Because all the motorcycles with their laughter
Will not let them sleep. The robins say
It is spring, and red wings
And motorcycles are chattering,
Gas tanks and distinct calls
Shaped like tears of blood.

## The Philosopher Savant Hears Piano Music Climbing, 9:41 PM

I straighten my back on the mattress.
I yawn. The music says, "It's all you've
Done; it's all you've done." It climbs
To the corner of the room like a spider
And falls. Today is my daughter Julia's
Birthday. It is cloudy and cars sound
Muffled as they drive by as if
Covered in green wool. Some messages
Come to me from the horizon:
There was a church built near the reservoir,
But when we walked there again, it was gone.
I looked up and there was a river
Where the playground once was.
Far away, there was a swirl of trees.

## Acknowledgments

"The Philosopher Savant Takes a Walk" originally appeared in *The New Yorker* on January 13, 2014. Other poems appeared in *The American Poetry Journal*, *Verse Daily*, *Illya's Honey*, *Cedar Valley Divide*, *Poetry East*, *California Quarterly*, *Lyrical Iowa*, *Pirene's Fountain*, *Levure Litteraire*, *The Briar Cliff Review*, *The Contemporary Review*, & *Fact of the Universe*. Infinite thanks to the editors for publishing these poems.

# About the Author

**Rustin Larson's** poetry has appeared in *The New Yorker, The Iowa Review, North American Review, Poetry East,* and *The American Entomologist Poet's Guide to the Orders of Insects.* He is the author of *The Wine-Dark House* (Blue Light Press, 2009), *Crazy Star* (selected for the Loess Hills Book's Poetry Series in 2005), and *Bum Cantos, Winter Jazz, & The Collected Discography of Morning,* winner of the 2013 Blue Light Book Award (Blue Light Press, San Francisco).

# Glass Lyre Press

exceptional works to replenish the spirit

Glass Lyre Press is an independent literary publisher interested in technically accomplished, stylistically distinct, and original work. Glass Lyre seeks diverse writers that possess a dynamic aesthetic and an ability to emotionally and intellectually engage a wide audience of readers.

Glass Lyre's vision is to connect the world through language and art. We hope to expand the scope of poetry and short fiction for the general reader through exceptionally well-written books, which evoke emotion, provide insight, and resonate with the human spirit.

Poetry Collections
Poetry Chapbooks
Select Short & Flash Fiction
Anthologies

www.GlassLyrePress.com

www.ingramcontent.com/pod-product-compliance
Lightning Source LLC
Chambersburg PA
CBHW021159080526
44588CB00008B/414